CW00704675

EAT GEORGIAN FEEL GOOD

VEGAN AND VEGETARIAN RECIPES

FROM HELENA

HELENA BEDWELL
EAT GEORGIAN, FEEL GOOD

Second edition, 2019

Edited by Mark Beech
Designed by Gastronaut

Illustrations by Davina Bedwell
Photographs & Food styling by Emma Matevosyan, in collaboration with Gastronaut
Cover Photo by Goga Chanadiri

DEDICATED TO MY CHILDREN
IAN AND DAVINA BEDWELL

Helena Bedwell is a veteran journalist of 25 years.

She lives in Norfolk (UK) and Tbilisi Georgia.

This is her second cookery book after
Flavours from Helena'. Her career has
several countries. During this period, she
in addition to her written journalistic
in 1998 with her British husband, they
but Helena never stopped her career,
Georgian food and promoting it. Now she
financial news company, where she has
Her stories have appeared live on
has mostly reported on financial stories,
economy, lifestyle and banking in
development and psychology
translator and

a successful launch of the 'Georgian
been varied because she has lived in
has applied her skills as a TV reporter
accomplishments. After leaving Georgia
travelled the world with their children,
and also, developed an interest in cooking
works for Bloomberg News, a worldwide
successfully worked for the last 11 years.
Bloomberg TV programmes, and she
concentrating on the government, the
Georgia. Helena also holds child
diplomas and is a certified
interpreter.

Contents

FRESH STARTERS ---------- 15
Shredded Aubergines ---------- 16
Abaklajanchpa ---------- 18
Simple Wild Ghandzili ---------- 20
Cabbage Parcels ---------- 22
Lobio (Beans) Kirkazhi Style ---------- 24

Georgian Pkhali Platter ---------- 27
Red Spinach or Beetroot Pkhali ---------- 28
Spinach or Chard Pkhali ---------- 29
Green Beans with Walnuts ---------- 30
Leek Pkhali ---------- 31

HOT VEGGIE MAINS ---------- 33
Lobio (Bean) Soup Kakhuri ---------- 34
Tbilisi Ajafsandali ---------- 36
Nittikhingal ---------- 38
Kharcho with Mushrooms ---------- 40

SALADS ---------- 43
Cucumber and Tomato Salad ---------- 44
Beetroot Salad Barbare Style ---------- 46
My Dad's Green Salad with Cucumbers ---------- 48
Akhali Potato Salad ---------- 50

GEORGIAN FASTING DELIGHTS ---------- 53
Lentil Stew ---------- 56
Buckwheat Soup ---------- 57

Heavenly Desserts from Mother Elisabeth ---------- 59
Carrot Dessert ---------- 62
Korkoti Wheat Dessert ---------- 63
'Mother Elisabeth' Energy Drink ---------- 64
'Mother Elisabeth' Energy Bites ---------- 65

VEGGIE SAUCES ---------- 67

Marinia's Tkemali ---------- 68
Cauliflower in Bajhe ---------- 70
Ajika ---------- 72
Blackberry Sauce ---------- 74
Niortskali ---------- 74
Garlic Water ---------- 74

CARB FIXES ---------- 77

Diamond-Shape Mchadis ---------- 78
Ghomi ---------- 80
Rice or Semolina Ghomi ---------- 81
Adjarian 'Boats' ---------- 82
Puff Pastry Lobiani ---------- 84
Mom's Stuffed Vegetables ---------- 86
Chaqapuli ---------- 88

MURABAS AND OTHER SWEETS ---------- 91

Crab Apple Muraba ---------- 92
Clementine Muraba ---------- 94
Fruit Churchkhela or Janjukha ---------- 96
Baked Apples with Dry Fruits ---------- 98

Foreword

It's been a great year! My first book, Georgian Flavours from Helena, was launched in Georgia and found its way to my close friends, relatives and foreigners who loved Georgia at first sight.

My concept is simple: a laid-back approach, which is a reflection of the Georgian approach to home cooking. This is how my mother, granny and aunt approached their kitchen.

As a passionate promoter of my country's cuisine, people naturally ask me about Georgian food. The most frequent question I hear is whether Mtsvadi or 'shish-kebab' in English (grilled meat or vegetables cooked over an open flame) and Khinkali (meat dumplings) are our most popular dishes. This is a myth, but these are the most common dishes to be found in Georgian restaurants, so the ones that tourists often talk about. They are also Soviet-era stereotypes.

However, in this extremely varied, agriculturally rich country, meat is mostly for special days, holidays and celebrations.

In reality, vegetables, fruits, nuts, herbs and cheese dominate the Georgian culinary repertoire. For example, Georgian cooking is abundant in walnut-based or infused dishes. Georgia is a veritable vegetarian and vegan heaven!

Another feature of Georgian cuisine is its versatility: no recipe is sacrosanct. All can be, and are, adapted to local produce, taking into account seasonal variations, the mood and the moment. The Georgian menu has been built up over thousands of years and continues to accommodate changing influences. While most dishes are simple, they reflect the tastes of the many invaders and travellers who have brought ideas here from all points of the compass – Europe, Russia, Asia and the Middle East.

Georgians, however, believe first in comfort food, avoiding typical incarnations of classical dishes from the Orient and Occident.

There is little to be found in Georgian restaurants that that is not also served on the table at home. Most importantly, those running the Georgian kitchen, be they mothers, aunts or grandmothers, also keep a watchful eye on their purses.

Vegetables dominate the markets as well as the menus, and the list of vegan and vegetarian dishes is astonishingly colourful.

Another feature of Georgian cooking is that you will find many ingredients that have been lost in other countries, victims of industrial-scale commercial agriculture. Yes, potatoes, beans and corn entered Georgia in the late middle centuries, but Georgians are also still using local rye, oats, lentils, millet, hedgerow herbs and ancient but healthier wheat varieties.

So when I was asked to participate in vegan and vegetarian food festivals in the U.K., I managed to supply my tables with a wide variety of vegan choices from Georgia without any trouble.

Many of our recipes have been with us for centuries, such as Pkhaleuli, (Vegetables with walnuts), Which historians agree were first consumed in the western part of the country. Practically any edible plant was used to make Pkhali, even nettles! Meanwhile, Georgian desserts were made mainly of honey and nuts.

The wide range of spicy food made from the local chilli came as a remedy to ward off malaria. Much of our food is based on what is good for people's health.

Why should Georgian vegetarian cuisine be interesting for the rest of the world? The past decade has seen Georgian tourism boom - everywhere you have look, whether, in the snow-capped mountains, woodlands, forests or the Black Sea, visitors have been flooding Georgia to enjoy the sightseeing, the wine and the culinary adventures.

The future for Georgian food is NOW! The time has come for the pkhali and walnut, aubergines, and green bean salads with pomegranate or kidney bean soup with pickles, and so on. In this book, I will try to teach and recreate recipes from my family cookbooks, some directly from historians and, for the secrets of the fasting menu, from Georgia's nuns and monks, who invented some of the most delicious dishes with which, religious or not, you will fall in love.

Georgia is an ancient, predominantly Orthodox Christian country where many people practice fasting four times a year. A Georgian fasting menu has so much in common with a vegan menu that vegans will be amazed.

The fasting periods are around Christmas, Easter, and the saints' days of St. Mary and St. Peter. Wednesdays and Fridays are also fasting days for many religious people. According to Georgian church rules, fish is allowed on certain fasting days. Of course, proteins such as beans, pulses and lentils are essential dishes for Georgians (and anyone else) who are fasting.

As in my first book, I want to highlight the tasty side of this small historic country. Non-Georgians love to explore the country's culinary expertise, and my recipes are written, so they are easy to grasp by anyone, regardless of age or gender. Modern Georgian cooking with organic food is much simpler than the dishes that our grandmothers made.

The amazing thing about Georgian cooking is that you can make delicious vegetarian and vegan dishes by just substituting vegetables for meat in so many dishes – there is no need to add processed vegan meat substitutes. So go for it and give it a try.

Georgian food is fun!

Useful Tricks from Helena

- Old Georgians used to eat Khmiadi (shown in the picture with soups), a flat dry bread which was easy to store and made inside the fireplace sprinkled with flamed wood chippings You can either use flat 'lavash' bread (a Western Asian and Middle Eastern alternative) or make your own with plain wheat flour and water, adding salt. Do not use yeast.
- Use flat lavash pieces of bread to pan-fry with several filling inside such as vegan cheese, spinach or herbs of your choice.
- Ingredients a good blender to make a walnut paste, as the old (mortar and pestle) method will take a long time. Place the walnuts, garlic and spices together with vinegar and water in a blender to make the walnut paste. Blend well, and you will get a nice thick yellowish aromatic paste.
- I have successfully used the almond paste to create Georgian dishes. Feel free to do so.
- Use vegan oils or any organic vegetable oils. Georgians use sunflower and corn oil when cooking or to drizzle over salads.
- Use coconut oil instead of normal oil, although it is not a very Georgian thing to do.
- Maple syrup and Agave nectar can replace honey and sugar.
- To make Mchadi, you need a good coarse corn flour. Mazeca would do just fine because Georgian milled corn is not available in Europe. An alternative Georgian homemade method is to use boiled rice and then mixed with cornflour to make polenta.
- Varieties of spices are available to buy, such as blue fenugreek, yellow flower, KhmeliSuneli (Georgian spice mix at its best) and Svanetian Salt, but feel free to use any of your vegan-approved spices. The yellow flower we know, also called Imere-

tian Saffron, but it is not the well-known Safron. It's unique. So is Gitsruli, one of the main components of the Svanetian Salt mix, locally called the wild coriander. Old recipes also included cannabis seed, not widely used now of course.

- Wild garlic, called Ghandzili in Georgia, is hard to get abroad. Swap it with leek.

- When making Lobio, which is a bean stew, drop into the pan half a lemon or lemon juice while boiling. It will help to remove toxins from the beans. Also, it's a good idea to eat Lobio with something sour, like pickled cucumbers.

- Georgians love homemade white wine vinegar. Apple vinegar can be a suitable substitute.

- If you prepare Ajika (Georgian chilli) sauce beforehand and store it in the fridge, then cooking is easier. Then you can add it to any dishes when cooking as an alternative to spices and herbs.

- Do not be afraid to use ready-made garlic pastes or other sauces to save time.

- There is a wide range of vegan and vegetarian pastries or vegan cheeses already prepared which are available to use.

- Make a Georgian vegetarian or vegan dinner for four or six, or simply serve it as a platter for a starter, and follow it with two hot dishes served with polenta or Mchadi. Georgians lay the table as a mix of many dishes - the objective being to cover the table with dishes - rather than serve the dishes individually to each person.

- Ginger, lemon, lime or other exotic ingredients can be added if desired.

- Vinegar can be replaced with lemon juice.

- It's OK to use freshly frozen vegetables if you wish.

- Honey is a hot topic among vegans, but there are plenty of bee-free honey options are available to use in the recipes to replace honey.

- Old Georgia's used so-called GhomisGhomi (Foxtail Millet) to make polenta. The endemic variety is not wide-spread today if at all. Georgians today make polenta using cornflour and even rice.

- Finally, a toast to the best 'Georgian moments.'

FRESH STARTERS

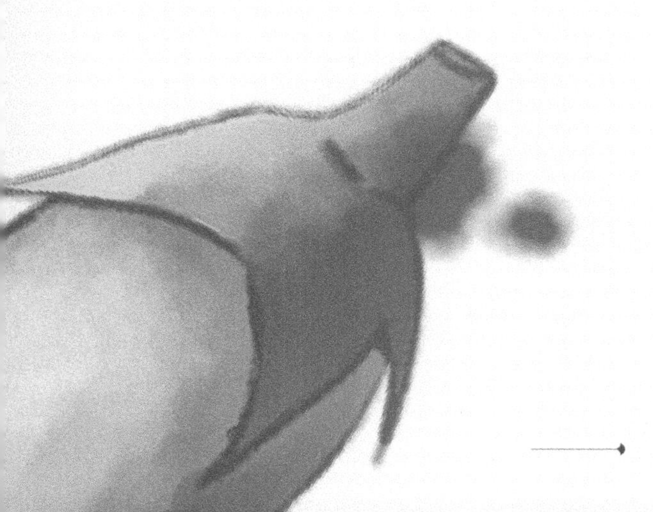

SHREDDED AUBERGINES

აკენკილი ბადრიჯანი

 *15 mins.* *4-6 pers.*

Ingredients:

500 g of large aubergines;
250 g of walnuts;
A few cloves of garlic;
2 tbsp. of sunflower oil;
Parsley;
1 tsp. of chilli or fresh chilli;
Some dry spices, such as coriander;
3 tbsp. of vinegar;
Salt as desired;
Pomegranate and herbs to decorate.

How to prepare:

I find that baking aubergines in the oven work better than frying for this dish because the slices come out drier. But if you prefer an oilier version, then fry them.

Before frying the aubergines, sprinkle with salt to remove some of the moisture. Make sure they are browned well and as soon as the slices have cooled, separate them into long strips.

Start preparing the walnut paste while the aubergines are cooling down. Combine walnuts, finely chopped onion and coriander at first and blend. Add blue fenugreek, dry parsley, yellow flower, chilli powder and salt. The paste is ready. Add a tiny bit of water to make it more liquid if you like.

Put the strips into a large bowl and mix with a wooden spoon, slowly adding the walnut paste. You may add pomegranate seeds inside the dish, or place some on top, and sprinkle generously with chopped herbs.

ABAKLAJANCHPA

(Abkhazian version)

აბაკლაჟანჩპა

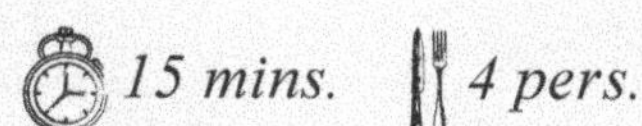

Ingredients:

3 large aubergines;
3 large red and green peppers;
250 g of walnuts or almonds;
Cloves of garlic, crushed;
Oil of your choice in the quantity you prefer;
1 tbsp. of chilli or fresh chilli;
Some dry spices, such as coriander;
Fresh herbs;
3 tbsp. spoon of vinegar;
Salt as desired.

How to prepare:

This Abkhazian dish is slightly different from the well-known aubergine rolls and stringy aubergines because it looks more like a salad. The method is almost the same, but the aubergine pieces are chunkier.

Fry the aubergine slices and then cut them into cubes. Chop sweet peppers and fry them too, then mix with the aubergines. Toss in walnuts (which can be optional), peppers and all the other ingredients to make the salad. If you want the salad to be spicier, add chilli to the vinegar before dressing the salad. Serve cold.

SIMPLE WILD GHANDZILI

ღანძილი

Ghandzili is a Georgian word for wild garlic. It has a very specific taste and flavour, so if you find it's hard to get, or it is out of season, simply use leeks instead.

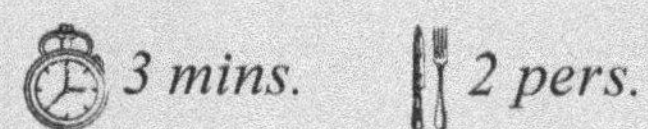

Ingredients:

300 g of Ghandzili or leeks;
1 bunch of coriander;
Salt, thick oil and vinegar to taste.

How to prepare:

Pre-soak the wild garlic or leeks in boiling water for five minutes. Take it out, drain it in a colander and shred by hand. Season with vinegar, coriander and salt, or with pomegranate juice. Serve with cornbread (See recipe on page 78) as shown in the picture.

➔ Asparagus is another old endemic variety; some of my relatives used it in this recipe successfully.

CABBAGE PARCELS

კომბოსტოს რულეტი

Ingredients:

1 whole small cabbage;
Cloves of garlic;
A few tbsp. of sunflower oil;
200 g of walnuts;
1 tsp. blue fenugreek mix;
1 tsp. of dried chilli or fresh chilli;
Some dry spices, such as coriander;
Parsley, dry and fresh;
3 tbsp. of vinegar;
Salt as desired;
Pomegranate and herbs to decorate.

How to prepare:

This starter was always my mom's favourite dish and fun to make. She used to make it close to the New Year celebrations.

Soak the cabbage leaves in boiled oily water or place the cabbage into a half-filled pot of simmering water till tender. Meanwhile, make the paste.

The walnut paste is made the same way as described above for other starters. For this dish, we recommend walnuts, not almonds.

Place the paste inside the flattened cabbage leaf. This can be tricky until you get the hang of it because the paste must be slightly runnier to soak the cabbage leaf.

Spread the cabbage leaf evenly with the walnut paste and then roll into a log shape. You can then decide whether you want to cut the roll into smaller pieces or serve as a long roll. Arrange the cabbage starters on the plate and sprinkle generously with some pomegranate seeds and herbs. I find that dry redcurrants are also suitable for this dish as a decoration.

LOBIO (BEANS) KIRKAZHI STYLE

კირკაჟი ლობიო

The word Kirkazhi or Kvarkvala originates from the round shape of girls' eyes and is the slang word for 'large eyes'. So, as the word indicates, you should use large round kidney beans.

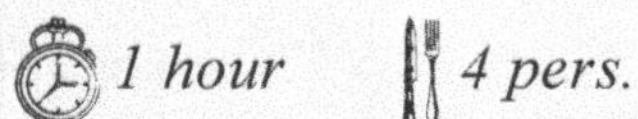

1 hour *4 pers.*

Ingredients:

400 g of beans (lobio);
1 bunch of coriander;
1 bunch of parsley;
1 teaspoon of dry oregano;
0.5 teaspoons of chilli;
3 or 4 teaspoons of oil;
4 onions;
1 large red sweet pepper;
Salt and pepper to taste.

How to prepare:

Boil the beans until cooked. Chop the onions along with sweet pepper and sauté them. Chop the coriander and parsley and add them to the onions with the other ingredients. Pour this mixture over the boiled and drained beans. Add some vinegar and flavoured oil, preferably unrefined. Best served with cornbread as shown in the picture.

Georgian Pkhali Platter

Pkhali is the star of any Georgian table. The collection of patés can be arranged in various shapes, like balls, ovals or small plates. Each can be seen served as an appetizer before every Georgian meal with the must-have accompaniment of Mchadi (cornbread).
The secret is to keep them chilled before serving and decorate them with fresh herbs, pomegranate seeds. Cornbread perfectly complements it, and you hardly need anything else, except maybe a glass of wine!
There is nothing more beautiful and tastier than a selection of Georgian pkhali (Vegetable spread with walnut pâté) arranged nicely on a wooden platter, garnished with herbs, pomegranate seeds, onion rings and served with crispy hot bread or Mchadi (cornbread).
Georgians also serve the platter along with some pickles and cheese slices.

We arranged the pkhali platter in this picture together served with fresh herbs and cornbread.

RED SPINACH OR BEETROOT PKHALI

წითელი ფხალი

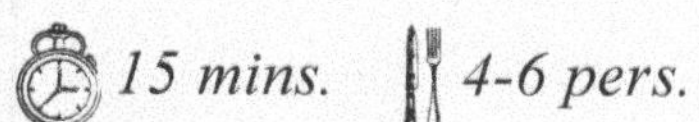

Ingredients:

1 kg fresh red spinach or beetroot;
200 g of chopped walnuts (almonds can also be used);
3 cloves of garlic;
Few tbsps. of sunflower oil;
1 tsp. of dried chilli or fresh chilli;
Some dry spices, such as coriander;
Parsley, dry and fresh;
1 tbsp. of marigold, dried (calendula);
3 tbsp. of vinegar;
Salt as desired;
Pomegranate and herbs to decorate.

How to prepare:

Both red spinach or beetroot are ideal for this dish. It's a great festive and colourful dish to serve for any season, and tasty too.
Bring a large pan of water to the boil. Reduce the heat and soak the leaves. Boil until tender, poking it from time to time to test that they are cooked. (As the pieces will be pureed, appearance does not matter.) Alternatively, baking them is also a good idea.
Meanwhile, make the paste in the food processor, adding all the spice ingredients together with the walnuts. Making the paste should take about five minutes because it must be smooth and not chunky. I find that adding a bit of boiled water also helps give the paste a good consistency.
Take out the boiled pieces of pumpkin or butternut squash and mash them with a fork. Do not blend in the food processor, because they need to have a stringy appearance.
Now mix all the ingredients and garnish with pomegranate seeds or herbs. I find this dish is appealing served either warm or cold.

→ The beetroot version is prepared the same way.

SPINACH OR CHARD PKHALI

მწვანე ფხალი

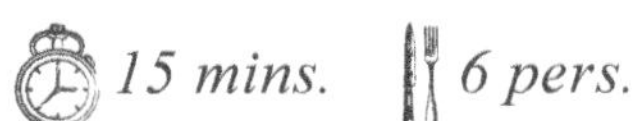

Ingredients:

1 kg fresh spinach or chard;
200 g of chopped walnuts;
3 cloves of garlic;
3 onions chopped;
A few tbsps. of sunflower oil;
1 tsp. of chilli or fresh chilli;
Some dry spices, such as coriander;
Parsley, dry and fresh;
1 tbsp. of marigold (calendula), dried;
3 tbsp. of vinegar;
Salt as desired;
Pomegranate seeds to garnish.

How to prepare:

Bring a large pan of water to boil and add the green leaves. Cook for a minute or so until they have softened enough to be pliable. (Remember every green plant of your choice takes a different time to boil.)

When ready, drain them in the colander and set aside until cool enough for you to handle. When ready, take handfuls (amounts like snowballs) and squeeze hard to drain any excess water. Then chop the leaves finely and leave to settle while you are making the walnut paste.

Walnut paste is made by the same method in a food processor, slowly adding all the remaining ingredients. You can sauté the onions, or if you want, you can use spring onions. Cook them separately in oil and set them aside to mix in later.

Take the chopped spinach and mix well by hand with the walnut. Adjust the consistency, if you wish. Add the sautéed onions and either serve made into small balls or lay flat on a nice serving plate, decorated with pomegranate seeds. Many cooks in Georgia make tiny bird-nest shaped balls out of the green Pkhali and put the seeds in as eggs.

Both chard or spinach, or even leeks, are suitable to make this green starter. My grandmother even used to use nettles. Of course, it is up to you to exercise your imagination and use the plant of your choice. The secret is to use your hands when making this Pkhali because it requires a lot of playing around to absorb the flavours of the spices.

GREEN BEANS WITH WALNUTS

მწვანე ლობიო

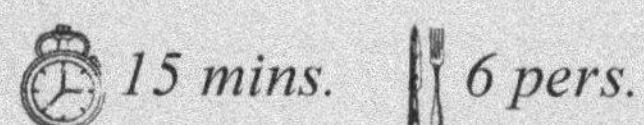

Ingredients:

1 kg of green string beans;
Basil or oregano of your choice;
Green peppers and spring onions.

How to prepare:

Boil the string beans, and when they are cooked, drain them and let them cool down. Press them by hand to remove the moisture. If beans are way too stringy to be used whole, they can be processed through the food processor. All remaining ingredients are tossed in with the beans before serving.

LEEK PKHALI

პრასი

Ingredients:

1 kg fresh leek;
200 g of chopped walnuts (almonds can also be used);
3 cloves of garlic;
A few tbsps. of sunflower oil;
1 tsp. of dried chilli or fresh chilli;
Some dry spices, such as coriander;
Parsley, dry and fresh;
1 tbsp. of marigold, dried (calendula);
3 tbsp. of vinegar;
Salt as desired;
Pomegranate and herbs to decorate.

How to prepare:

Bring a large pan of water to the boil. Reduce the heat and put the chopped or whole leeks in the pan. Soak until tender - 20 minutes approximately.

Meanwhile make the paste in the food processor, adding all the spice ingredients together along with the walnuts. Making the paste should take about five minutes because it must be smooth and not chunky. I find that adding a bit of boiled water also helps give the paste a good consistency.

Take out the soaked leek pieces and set to cool down. Do not blend in the food processor, because they need to have a stringy appearance.

Now mix all the ingredients and garnish with pomegranate seeds or herbs. I find the dish is appealing served either warm or cold.

HOT VEGGIE MAINS

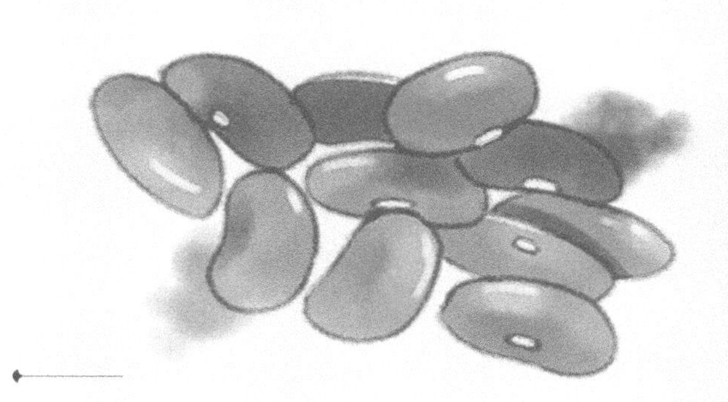

LOBIO (BEAN) SOUP KAKHURI

კახური ლობიო

 *1-2 hours.* *6 pers.*

Ingredients:

1 kg red kidney beans (canned ones can be used);
3 large onions;
Coriander;
Celery (fresh);
Salt and pepper to taste;
Garlic;
Heavy vegetable oil.

How to prepare:

Preparation and cooking time: 2 hours when the dry kidney beans are used, but 1 hour if you are using tinned beans

Pre-soak the red kidney beans the night before. (Obviously, canned beans won't require pre-soaking.) Boil the beans but pour out the water the first time it boils, add more water and continue to boil.

Separately, chop the onions and herbs and sauté them in a frying pan until soft. When the beans are ready, pour the onions and herbs onto them and mix well. Add salt and pepper as you wish, and serve with pickles, chilli or hot cornbread. Try the dish served with capers and pomegranates.

It was not an easy task to combine vegetarian and vegan cuisine with heavy Kakhetian vintage wine. So I had to go and ask an expert, someone like Shalva Khetsuriani, a dedicated wine-maker and the president of the Georgian Sommelier Association.

Marani Khetsuriani is a winery established in Kutaisi by Bakhva Khetsuriani in 1860, and production was restored by the sixth generation of his family in 1998 after the Soviet occupation was over.

Shalva told me that Lobio is not as popular in Kakheti as it is in the Imereti region, as food is heavier there compared to western Georgia. Shalva found it challenging to match lobio with Kakhetian wine. The traditional Saperavi, one of their first vintages in 1999 from the Akhasheni vineyard, is matched with Lobio to make it more palatable.

SAPERAVI
HETSOURIANI
1999

TBILISI AJAFSANDALI

თბილისი აჯაფსანდალი

My foodie advisor and Professor Dalila Tsathba tells me, this is a real Tbilisi dish. Served hot or cold, it's a true joy for vegetable lovers, as well as a substantial dish for non-vegetarians.

 *45 mins.* *4-6 pers.*

Ingredients:

500-600 g of aubergines;
5 carrots;
4-5 sweet peppers;
4-5 potatoes (or you may use sweet potatoes if you wish) soaked in boiling salty water to release the starch;
4-5 onions;
Fresh tomatoes and a tin of chopped tomatoes;
Green beans;
Fresh herbs such as coriander, parsley or basil;
A few cloves of garlic;
Salt and pepper as desired.

How to prepare:

Take the aubergines and cut them into long slices. After they have been sliced, place the pieces in a bowl and sprinkle with salt. This will allow the aubergines to release any extra moisture, so they won't get overcooked or absorb too much oil. Leave to stand for at least 30 minutes or so.

Fry the onions until they are lightly browned. Add the aubergines and potatoes. Continue to simmer, slowly adding all the other remaining ingredients, until the vegetables are nicely mixed and softened. Add tomatoes, fresh first and then the tinned tomatoes, cover and continue to simmer. Add salt and pepper, and any other spice you may find interesting, while slowly mixing.

Sprinkle with chopped fresh herbs before serving.

Enjoy.

→ My mother and auntie used to add a cup of pre-soaked white rice to this dish. Why not try the same? Brown rice also works.

You may add any other vegetable to this recipe. I have added cauliflower and zucchini on occasions, and both worked well with the rest of the colours.

NITTIKHINGAL

ნითინგხინგალ

If you drive to the eastern part of Georgia, towards the northern border with Chechnya, in the Akhmeta area, you'll find a group of picturesque villages, home to the Kists, an ethnic group that traces its origins back to the Chechens. Breathtakingly well-kept houses feature in this region, with large front yards.
In the area of the Pankisi Gorge, locals make the most exquisite cheese, which is available throughout Georgia. Nobody goes hungry in this region.
I've met some powerful women here, two of whom won a local TV cooking show. However, my inspiration from this region was Naira, the mother of my friend Sulkhan, who taught me how to prepare local dishes. Here is one that uses a favourite plant of mine - the nettle.

 *1 hour* *5-10 pers.*

Ingredients:
1 kg nettles;
50 g flour per kilo of nettle;
Oil and salt.

How to prepare:
Use gloves when pre-washing and soaking the nettles in boiling water for 3 minutes. Then the nettles should be sautéed lightly with oil and salt.
Separately, make a dough using flour and half a litre of lukewarm water. The dough may take some time. Flatten it and cut out it out into round shapes using a cup. The round shapes must not be too thick when pressing by hand, or they will split during the boiling. Medium consistency would be fine. Place tiny dots of nettle on each shape. Wrap each piece of dough into a pouch and finish by seeing how many wrinkles you can make around the edges - the more, the merrier. Drop the pouches into boiling salty water; they are done when they float to the surface.

→ You may simply use mushroom or spinach filling instead of nettle to simplify the recipe but the original Pankisi treat is with the nettle.

KHARCHO WITH MUSHROOMS

სოკოს ხარჩო

This dish is normally made with meat, but I have recreated it using mushrooms. You can also use courgettes or aubergines, substituting them for the mushrooms. However, I highly recommend the mushroom version.

 *45 mins.* *6 pers.*

Ingredients:

One onion;
1 kg Mushroom mix of your choice;
180 g walnuts;
2 tsp. blue fenugreek;
1 tsp. dry coriander;
Half tsp. yellow flower (Imeretian Saffron);
Salt and pepper to taste;
1 tbsp. red ajika;
1 large pomegranate.

How to prepare:

Preheat the oil in a saucepan. Chop the mushrooms and sliced onion in rings and cook for five minutes or so. Add salt to taste and then prepare the walnut paste.
Prepare the walnut paste as above, then add to the sautéed vegetables. Then, depending on your choice, either add liquid using water or one large pomegranate juice. The ajika is important to give it a spicy kick.

→ This dish is ideal served with the Georgian polenta. See Polenta recipe on Page 80-81.

SALADS

CUCUMBER AND TOMATO SALAD

ქართული სალათი

This salad is a Georgian signature dish. A simple but amazingly flavoured salad, it is easy to make, easy to serve, and a delight for vegetarians. There is a version with walnuts, which give it an extra boost, but those with nut allergies can leave these out. You can also add cheese.

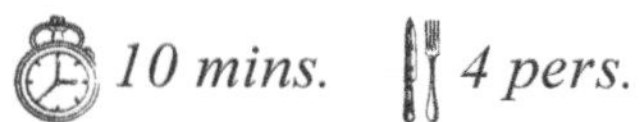 *10 mins.* 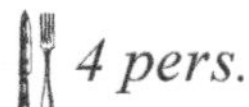 *4 pers.*

Ingredients:

1-2 long cucumbers;
6 small or 3 large tomatoes;
1 large onion;
Fresh herbs of your choice, I use blue basil;
1 tbsp. of thick sunflower oil;
Drizzle of vinegar;
A handful of crushed or chopped walnuts (optional);
Salt and pepper.

How to prepare:

Cut the cucumbers and tomatoes into slices. You can peel the cucumbers if you like. It's best to mix the ingredients by hand, slowly adding the seasoning. Serve chilled.

➔ If you serve the salad without adding walnuts, add more sunflower oil and vinegar. For a non-vegan option, add some mozzarella or any cheese of your choice.

BEETROOT SALAD BARBARE STYLE

ბარბარეს ჭარხალი

One of Georgia's most important contributors to our knowledge of Georgian cuisine was Barbare Jorjadze, an 18th Century Georgian princess, author and women's rights advocate, one of Georgia's first feminists. She wrote the country's first-ever complete kitchen cookbook. She didn't use ingredient lists as such, simply describing how she added ingredients of one sort or another as she went along. So we will keep to her style, and you can fill in any gaps by using your imagination.

 *25 mins.* *2 pers.*

Ingredients:

One large beetroot;
Vinegar;
Mustard;
Salt and pepper.

How to prepare:

Bake or boil the beetroot. Peel off the skin and place the beets in a bowl. Put some mustard and pepper with vinegar, salt and a bit of sugar in water and boil together. When this has cooled, pour over the beetroot slices. You can create a tower out of the vegetables by placing them in a form. Decorate it with herbs.

MY DAD'S GREEN SALAD WITH CUCUMBERS

მამას სალათი

This was my father's summer trademark. He loved to pick green salad leaves and cucumbers from our countryside garden and toss the salad with plenty of vinegar and spring onions.

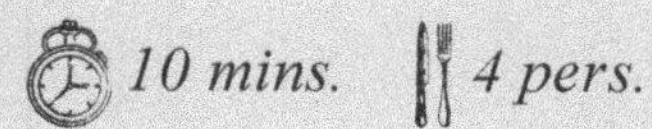

Ingredients:

One large head of green salad leaves;
3 large cucumbers;
Bunch of spring onions;
Apple cider vinegar or any vinegar;
Black pepper to season.

How to prepare:

Rinse the leaves and dry. Chop the salad leaves or break them by hand into a bowl. Add cucumbers chopped in rings and spring onions.

Add plenty of vinegar and toss before adding pepper. My dad never used oil for this recipe, but feel free to do so.

AKHALI POTATO SALAD

ახალი კარტოფილი

The name 'Akhali' means new. This is a hot salad, made of baby potatoes and a spring delight, especially with the addition of dill. This dish is, of course, known worldwide as well as on the Georgian table. To make them extra-delicious, the potatoes can be dipped in local sauces.

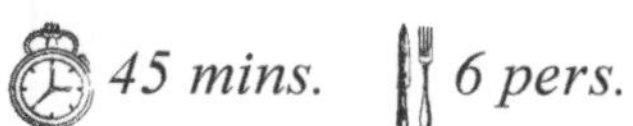

Ingredients:

20 tiny potatoes;
6 tbs of chopped fresh dill;
Salt and black pepper;
Several tbsp. of cooking oil of your choice.

How to prepare:

Wash, scrub and dry the tiny potatoes. Put them in a large casserole dish or frying pan with salt and pepper and cov-er. Cook about for 45 minutes, shaking occasionally. They are done when you can pierce them with the tip of a sharp knife.

Toss the chopped fresh dill and serve hot. Best served with Tkemali sauce. See Tkemali recipe on Page 68.

GEORGIAN FASTING DELIGHTS

Georgia is a religious country, therefore Lent is widely observed, and the church expects Christians to abstain from eating meat, eggs and dairy products. At these times Georgians' staple diet is the vegetable dishes, particular Pkhaleluli. This is a traditional Georgian dish of chopped and minced vegetables, made of cabbage or eggplant, spinach, beans, beets and others combined with ground walnuts, vinegar, onions, garlic, and herbs. (Pkhali is also called mkhali). The common ingredient of all variations of pkhali is pureed walnut sauce.

Every household or a restaurant has its way of serving this dish, and everyone from tourists to professional gourmets loves them all. You can make them with vegetables of your choice. I find the tastiest with spinach, pumpkin, butternut squash, aubergines, chard or green string beans. Why don't you come up with something on your own; maybe your country has a vegetable in season? Try!

I am grateful of Protobespiteros Giorgi Zviadadze to introduce me to a wonderful Georgian nun, Mother Elisabeth, who told me: "Walnuts must be taken lightly: five pieces are enough per day, it is the queen of our table, but we avoid it."

LENTIL STEW

ოსპის წვნიანი

One of the old folk tales I read, mentions the man who comes home from a hard day working in the field and tell his wife to make him a Lentil Stew, which meant how popular it was and meant as a well-nourished meal

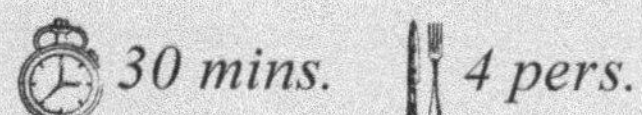

Ingredients:

One onion, chopped;
Corn oil (for preference);
2 garlic cloves;
Red pepper for the colour;
250 g lentils;
Coriander, rosemary;
Water;
Salt and pepper as desired;
Sautee.

How to prepare:

Pour oil in a soup pot, add the chopped onions and garlic and cover and cook over medium heat until tender and lightly coloured. This should take about 15 minutes,
Then add the lentils and continue to simmer, slowly add water, herbs, and chopped red peppers, salt and pepper bring to the boil. Reduce the heat, cover and simmer for another 20 minutes.
Remove from the heat and cool. Transfer to a blender and puree the mixture to the desired consistency. Adjust the seasoning to taste before serving.

➜ In this recipe, the lentils are blended, but to make the non-blended version, simply pre-soak the lentils for 3-6 hours then boil for 20 minutes maximum and add sautéed onions, garlic and mustard with salt. The simple Shechamandi (Georgian word for a stew) is still used widely during the fasting season.

BUCKWHEAT SOUP

წიწიბურას წვნიანი

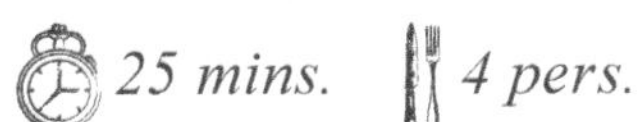

Ingredients:

200 g of mushrooms of your choice;
Mushroom or vegetable stock;
100 g of buckwheat;
50 g of lemon juice;
50 g of soy;
5 cloves of garlic;
10 g of spring onions;
20 g of parsley;
20 g of tarragon;
Salt and pepper.

How to prepare:

At first sauté the onions lightly in the oil of your choice, add mushrooms, vegetable or mushroom stock and let it boil on a low heat until the mushrooms are soft.
Add the buckwheat and continue to boil with salt and pepper. Simmer for another 10 minutes.
Add garlic, spring onions and the other remaining herbs to the ready soup and serve warm with either dry Georgian bread, Khmiadi, or crackers.

➔ Chef Meriko tells me that mushrooms are used for the soup, but if preferred you can use vegetable mixes such as carrots, broccoli and even sweet peppers.

Heavenly Desserts from Mother Elisabeth

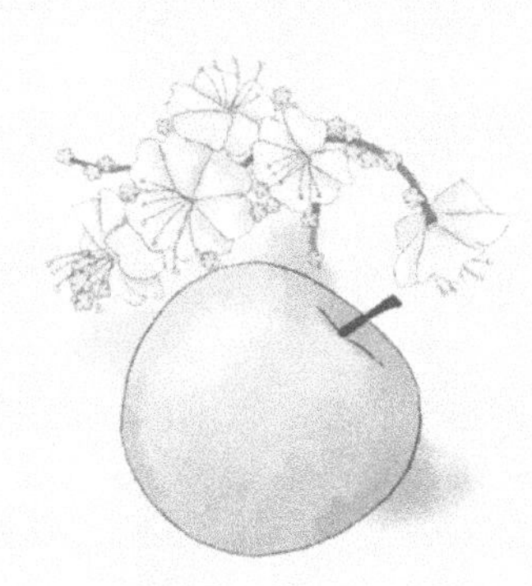

CARROT DESSERT

გახეხილი სტაფილო

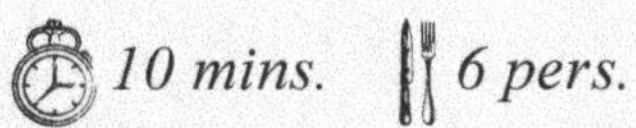

Ingredients:

5 grated raw carrots;
2 tbsps. red wine;
1 tbsp. honey or honey substitute;
A few dates;
5 almonds, flaked;
Add mint or dill on top.

How to prepare:

Grate the five raw carrots. Add the honey, a drizzle of red wine, the dates and almond flakes, and mix well. Taste and then keep in the fridge in whatever forms you like to shape them. Add mint on top for decoration before serving. Ideal as a healthy alternative dessert.

KORKOTI WHEAT DESSERT

კორკოტი

Ingredients:

Cinnamon;
Walnuts must be fresh and crunchy;
Honey;
Powdered sugar;
2 kg of wheat;
120 g of vegan butter;
150 g of sugar or honey;
1 teaspoon of walnuts roasted;
Handful of raisins.

How to prepare:

Pre-soak the wheat the night before. When it is fluffed up, then boil enough to press. It is a good idea to roast wheat after it has been pre-soaked overnight and before boiling it. Keep it boiling for two hours. Drain it using a colander and place the mix in a large bowl, adding sugar or honey, and then sprinkle walnuts and cinnamon over it.

'MOTHER ELISABETH' ENERGY DRINK

ტკბილი სასმელი

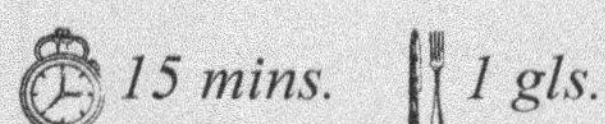

Ingredients:

Half a glass of water;
Half a glass of red, dry or semisweet wine;
One banana or orange;
Pinch of cinnamon and vanilla.

How to prepare:

As Mother Elisabeth tells me, this is the drink she consumes during Lent to keep her healthy.
Boil together the water and wine. Add the two chopped bananas, the vanilla and the cinnamon, and boil further for a few minutes.
This is served hot or cold to boost energy and makes four portions.

'MOTHER ELISABETH' ENERGY BITES

ტკბილი ბურთულები

Ingredients:

- 500 gr chopped walnuts;
- 1 tbsp. raisins;
- 100 g prunes;
- Honey;
- Lemon zest.

How to prepare:

All of the ingredients should be finely chopped and mixed with lemon zest, then they should be 'glued' together with boiled honey. Make the mixture into round shapes, dip them in cocoa or oil and then roll in cocoa powder. One a day supplies nearly all whole requirement of nutrients for a person who is fasting.

VEGGIE SAUCES

Georgian sauces are second to none! They are vegetarian and super healthy - Tkemali (plums, greengage sauce, ajika, and chilli paste), walnut, garlic, blackberry sauces, to name a few - and all can be served with any kind of dish, with vegetables, or with simple bread or cornbread. The uniqueness of these sauces means that they don't dilute or spoil the original flavour of dishes. On the contrary, they enhance them. They are easy to make and will amaze your guests.
Prepare a wholesome vegetable of your choice and pour the sauce over it. You will be amazed at how original the dish looks.

MARINIA´S TKEMALI

მარინიას ტყემალი

Marinia, as we call her at home, is my sparkly auntie who lives in the western part of Georgia. She is notorious for her sharp tongue and one of the best hostesses in the region of Vani. She certainly knows how to prepare this succulent Tkemali sauce!

 *20 mins.*

6 pers.

Ingredients:

3 kg of green-gages, or damsons (red or green);
5 bunches of coriander;
3 bunches of dill;
10 cloves of garlic;
Salt to taste.

How to prepare:

Boil the fruits in water.
When they have cooled, drain off the water using a colander.
All must be processed and added to the sieved tkemali juice. I love making this sauce. When abroad, I have found that large sweet plums are not quite suitable, but some of the red plum varieties, smaller in size and slightly sour are fine to use. The availability of greengages varies. For example, in Georgia, they are available from May until August, while I only found them in the U.K. during August.
Boil the fruits in a large, heavy pan. Simmer, until the plums start to peel, which shows they have softened enough. Then pour them into a large steel strainer placed over a large bowl or pan (which can be used again to boil the juices) and leave them to drain and cool down.
In my family, of course, we used our hands to squeeze the cooled plums through the strainer, especially as kids, when we loved to mess around with then. But use only a wooden spoon if you like to crush them. Once only the stones are left in the strainer, place the plums and juice over low heat. Leave it to simmer.
Meanwhile, mix the remaining ingredients by blending in the food processor. Combine with the plums and continue to simmer for another 10 minutes. Taste the mixture - if you feel it needs more salt or it's too sour, balance it with sugar or salt.
The Tkemali can be kept in the fridge for as long as 10 days. In Georgia, we store Tkemali in a dry, dark and cool place for the whole winter period. Bottle lids must be secure, and the mixture needs to be boiled again before storing.

CAULIFLOWER IN BAJHE

ბოსტნეული ბაჟეში

Bajhe is a walnut sauce, and is useful for any kind of dish, in our case vegetables. This is Dalila's sauce.

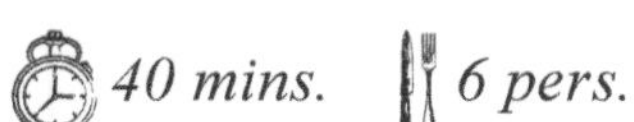

Ingredients:

150 g walnuts;
Red chilli;
4 cloves of garlic;
10 gr of blue fenugreek;
10 g dry coriander;
5 g marigold;
Salt according to taste;
300 ml water, pre-boiled.

How to prepare:

You will require a good blender for this one. Mix all the ingredients and add salt at the end or chilli if desired. Slowly add stock or water as you wish while keep stirring by hand or continue to blend.

Watch the consistency. You should be able to get a thick paste, which can be blended again, adding a teaspoon of warmed vinegar or pomegranate juice. I recommend using a wooden spoon when stirring by hand.

Make sure you are using mature garlic for this and not fresh. If you need the sauce for fish, add more coriander. The sauce also can be a delight for any vegetarian and vegan dish if you pour it over baked and fried vegetables, such as aubergine Bajhe or cauliflower Bajhe.

AJIKA

აჯიკა

Green

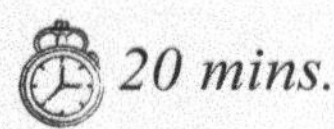 *20 mins.*

Ingredients:

300 g green, hot chillies;
50 g of garlic;
Coriander, parsley;
70 g + 50 dry coriander seeds + celery + green onion, spring onions;
50 g leeks;
30 g of salt;
Mint leaves;
Some crushed walnuts can be added if desired to give texture.

How to prepare:

All the ingredients should be blended, or put through a food processor bar the mint and walnuts. You can, if you like, remove the seeds from the chilis. Add the salt according to taste, and before serving add some oil and the crushed walnuts. This sauce will keep in the fridge for three weeks.

Red

 *20 mins.*

Ingredients:

300 g red chilli (possibly smoked for flavour);
70 g blue fenugreek;
30 g coriander;
10 g savoury herb;
300 g oil;
150 g salt;
80 g garlic.

How to prepare:

Make in the same way as the green ajika, but without walnuts.

BLACKBERRY SAUCE

მაყვლის წვენი

 *15 mins.*

Ingredients:
500 g of blackberries;
Small bunch of fresh coriander;
2-3 cloves of garlic;
Salt, pepper and chilli to taste.

How to prepare:
Crush the soft, well-ripened blackberries; use a sieve if you like. Then mix all the other remaining ingredients in a blender and add them to the blackberry sauce.
This sauce is ideal for all kinds of fish and vegetables of your choice. It can be poured over a dish.

NIORTSKALI
GARLIC WATER

ნიორწყალი

The main essence of this sauce is that it serves as a perfect flavour to augment any dish which has been fried or boiled. I use it, for example, to enliven a dish of beetroot.

 *15 mins.*

Ingredients:
5 cloves of garlic;
200 ml of boiled water.

How to prepare:
Crush the garlic and mix it well with the pre-boiled water. When you fry vegetables and spices, use the leftover cooking oil and some fried pieces that got stuck to the pan. It will give the garlic water a much better texture.

➔ One Georgian chef told me that sometimes he adds grated ginger to the sauce to give it a modern kick.

CARB FIXES

Mchadi (Cornbread)

Mchadi, the Georgian for cornbread, is one of my favourite, if not the most favourite, item on the Georgian table. Not only is this an amazing gluten-free alternative food to serve with starters or main dishes instead of wheat bread, but it's also healthy, tasty and it is what distinguishes Georgia from other cuisines that use cornflour in the kitchen.

DIAMOND-SHAPE MCHADIS

გრძელი მჭადი

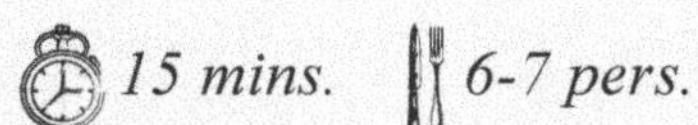

Ingredients:

500 g of cornflour;
Boiled water - as much as needed to create a soft and sticky, but not sloppy, dough.

How to prepare:

Take the cornflour, add a pinch of salt and bit of baking powder - but not too much (maybe a teaspoon full, but a small one). Add boiled water and stir carefully till you get a pliable dough. Make diamond or round shapes and bake them either in the oven or pan-fry on both sides.

GHOMI

(Georgian Polenta)

ღომი

This dish, a version of polenta, is a Georgian delight and ideal if you want a quick-carb fix. Make sure you prepare it inside a cast-iron pot to get the best results.

Normally Georgians mix it with cheese, but as a vegan option, it goes ideally with any of the sauces mentioned in this book or your sauce of choice. Also, one of the best versions I came across was with crushed walnuts and chilli.

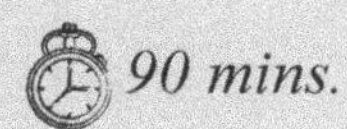
90 mins.

Ingredients:

300 g Ghergili (or coarse corn flour);

1 litre of water to make a simple polenta.

How to prepare:

Simply mix both ingredients and place them in a pan over medium heat, mixing constantly until it starts to thicken. Then leave to cook, further mixing from time to time until the smell of flour disappears, and the grains are soft.

Serving size not determined.

RICE OR SEMOLINA GHOMI

ბრინჯის ღომი

This is a very easy-to-do Ghomi to be made when Georgian Ghergilli(cornmeal) is not available. Simply replace the corn meal with corn flour and thicken the mixture with semolina or rice.

1 hour

Ingredients:

100 g of cornflour
400 g of semolina or white rice
2 litres of water

How to prepare:

Cover the cornflour with water and boil for at least 30 to 40 minutes. Stir periodically with a large wooden spoon. Mix with semolina or rice to thicken the mixture, but be careful not to get large lumps. Cook for another 25 minutes or so until the mixture is ready. For non-vegan dishes, add any cheese of your choice.

➔ Enjoy this dish cold the next day. Cut the leftover Ghomi into cubes, fry them in oil and dip them in any sauce like canapes.

Serving size not determined.

ADJARIAN 'BOATS'

აჭარული ბოსტნეულით

These are called 'Cheese Boats' because of their shape. In a restaurant, you would ask for an Adjarian Khachapuri, because it originates from the Georgian Black Sea region of Adjara. This is a must-have and there are two ways of enjoying it. There is quite a lot of bread, so you can either create a 'light' version by scooping out the soft dough (or asking the restaurant to do so) when it is cooked, leaving a very crispy (and healthier) crust. It's so much easier than to break off the crust to dunk chunks into the soft middle of cheese and egg. Or you can take it as it comes and enjoy the lot!

1 hour

Ingredients:

5 g of yeast diluted in water;
3 g of salt;
A bit of sugar
Warm water;
300-450 g of flour.

How to prepare:

Making the boat is fun! Fill it with anything you want - vegan cottage cheese, or kidney beans or red or green spinach, or Ajafsandali leftovers from our cookbook, for example. Consider this boat as your vessel to fill with anything you want from sweet to savoury flavours!

Start mixing the yeast with warm water, again with your hands. Add the salt and sugar to it. (The sugar will help the dough to go crisp in the oven.) Add flour and make a soft dough.

Mix ingredients at least 40 minutes to prepare the dough before baking. Alternatively, you can make it as early as possible to allow it to rise. When patting the dough, put some oil on your hands. This will allow you to play with it freely, and it won't stick to your hands.

Roll the dough into oval shapes first, and then start to fold both sides. You can make one or two folds and then secure the edges by sticking the dough together. Push the rolled sides apart, and you should be able to create a boat-like shape: practice makes perfect so that you can improvise.

Place the filling mixture in the middle of the boat and place it in the preheated oven. Ingredients 15 minutes to bake. Continue to bake until crispy and brown. A knob of vegan butter can be added later as desired.

One boat per serving

PUFF PASTRY LOBIANI

ფენოვანი ლობიანი

This is one of my favourite easy alternatives to the famous Khachapuri cheese bread. But instead of cheese, use beans; and instead of bread dough, use puff pastry for a crispy dish. The ready-made vegan pastry is widely available on the market.

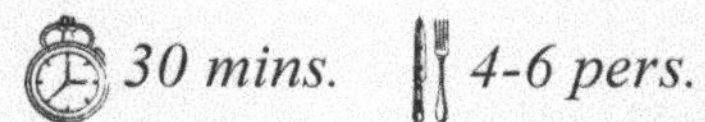

Ingredients:

1 roll of ready-made plain or vegan puff pastry;
500 gr of kidney beans or lobio soup leftovers.

How to prepare:

To prepare the bean filling, boil the kidney beans, drain them and mix with salt and pepper. Or simply use the recipe for bean soup, but drain it. so it is more like a paste.
Flatten the puff pastry ball or use the ready sheet of pasty. Sprinkle with flour and cut into four large or medium square pieces.
Place in the centre of each square a spoonful of bean paste balls and fold either like an envelope or into triangular pouches.
Bake the pouches in the oven till golden. Use non-animal oils to brush the tops a few minutes before they are done.

MOM'S STUFFED VEGETABLES

ბოსტნეულის ტოლმა

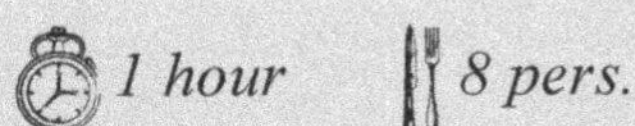

Ingredients:

500 g rice (white round or brown and wild mix);
8 sweet bell peppers of any colour;
1 large onion;
3 cloves of garlic;
6 large tomatoes;
6 aubergines;
1 green chilli;
50 ml of oil;
3 carrots;
Herbs: oregano, dill;
Salt and pepper as desired.

How to prepare:

Boil and drain the rice - don't over-boil it, because it will continue to cook inside the vegetables. Add one bunch of coriander, dill and oregano chopped.
Separately sauté the grated carrots, three chopped onions and three cloves of garlic in the sunflower or olive oil into the pan.
Clean the insides of the peppers and aubergines, and place in the boiling water to soften the skin then dry and stuff them with the rice mix.
Place the stuffed vegetables in the bottom of a large pan which has been filled with herb-infused water and which has been brought to the boil. Add the tomato and salt and boil for a further 10 minutes.
Alternatively, you can bake the stuffed peppers and aubergines in the oven.

CHAQAPULI

(Mushroom Stew with Greengage)

ჩაქაფული

This recipe was extremely popular in my first book, "Georgian Flavours from Helena". It is one of the most traditional Georgian recipes, served with loads of herbs in spring as a tonic after winter. The original is a very original, tangy lamb dish in which vegetarians and vegans can substitute mushrooms.

Georgians celebrate the ending of their Easter fasting with this dish. Greengages are widely available in Georgia at this time, but if you are abroad where it is too early in the year, and you cannot find any, try sour green plums (if they are available) or use greengage conserve.

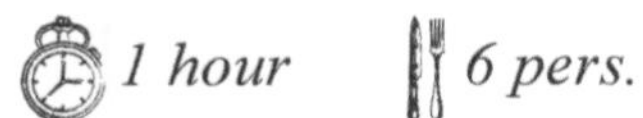

Ingredients:

1-2 kg large mushrooms;
300 g of coriander;
300 g spring onions;
300 g of tarragon;
Fresh stalks of wild garlic;
200 g of fresh greengages or Tkemali sauce;
Half a litre of dry white wine;
100 gr vegetable butter
Green pepper and salt to taste.

How to prepare:

Chop the mushrooms - in small cubes or however you like. Wash the herbs and then chop them all together.
In a large, deep saucepan, place some of the mushrooms at the bottom, sprinkle with herbs, then add another layer of mushrooms and then herbs, forming several layers. Then top up with butter, pepper, greengages or a greengage sauce and white wine and simmer on low heat.
When the mixture boils, season with salt, and continue to simmer. The dish is ready when the mushrooms are tender and soft. No need to add any water to this dish, because the white wine does the job!

➔ Use any mushrooms of your choice - White Button Mushrooms, Crimino Mushrooms, Portobello Mushrooms, Porcini or Oyster Mushrooms. Georgians often serve mushrooms baked simply in a clay pot, well-seasoned with cheese (optional). This is a fantastic combination with a glass of white wine.

MURABAS AND OTHER SWEETS

Georgia does not have many sweet dishes, but Muraba is a favourite. This is the Georgian name for a fruit conserve, and my country is unusual in the wide variety of this kind of fruit preserve that it makes. All fruits found in Georgia are made into Murabas, and sometimes vegetables as well - I have eaten delicious ones made with marrows - and a particularly unusual and delicious Muraba is made with rose petals.

A distinctive Georgian sweet is Churchkhela, which is made with strings of walnuts or hazel-nuts coated with grape juice thickened with cornflour. Traditionally, they are made in autumn when all the ingredients are fresh. No sugar is added, the grape juice supplying a natural sweetness. The combination is extremely nutritious, containing protein and vitamins. Georgian warriors used to carry strings of them attached to their waists as an easily portable food supply!

There is nothing nicer than homemade Murabas, and you can make good use of all fruits when they are in season. I have given just two recipes to show how they are made. Impress your guests with the Georgian sweet taste!

CRAB APPLE MURABA

სამოთხის ვაშლის მურაბა

My aunt Medea's trademark Muraba. She used to collect golden small apples in the village and make two versions of them. One part was used to decorate cakes and another part was for storing for winter.

2 hours

Ingredients:

1 kg of Apples;
1 kg Sugar;
300 g of water;
Lemon slices optional.

How to prepare:

Wash the apples well and place in the large pan. Pour in the sugar and ideally keep it overnight to release enough liquid from the apples.
Place it over low heat and bring to the boil.
Remove from the stove and place aside to cool down while well-covered.
As soon as it is cold, bring to the boil again and continue for a further 10 minutes.
The Muraba is ready to be distributed in small jars.

შავი ჩაი

CLEMENTINE MURABA

მანდარინის მურაბა

Tangerines and clementines are the most popular citrus fruits in the western seaside part of Georgia, especially in Abkhazia.
This recipe was given to me by the Abkhazian-origin chef, Guram Kiknadze.

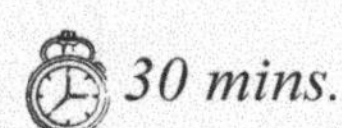

30 mins.

Ingredients:

1 kg of clementines
1 kg of sugar

How to prepare:

Remove the stalks, if any, and pierce the clementines in several places. Place them in the boiling water and let it continue to boil for five minutes. Then drain off that water, add the sugar and 275 g more water and continue to boil for another five minutes. Repeat at least three times. However, it is important to let the mixture cool several times, so as not to let it become caramelized.

ნარუჯა
მწვანე ჩა

FRUIT CHURCHKHELA OR JANJUKHA

ჩურჩხელა, ჯანჯუხა

My auntie Medea was not a big fan of the traditional Churchkhela made with walnuts with the coating mainly from the grape juice and wheat flour. In the part of Georgia she came from, Imereti, it is called Janjukha and is made with hazelnuts or dry fruits and corn meal. She made her own dried fruit, too, and after the apple harvest season she used to lay out chopped apple slices to dry in the sun. Sundried fruits are a softer alternative to traditional nuts and perfect for nut allergy sufferers.

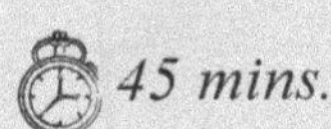

45 mins.

Ingredients:

1 litre of grape juice;
1.5 cups of cornflour;
2 tbsps. of plain white flour;
2 tbsps. of sugar;
Dry apples;
Thick string.

How to prepare:

Firstly, the coating: the flour should be mixed well with grape juice and sugar until it all dissolves. Or you can be non-traditional and use blackberry juice. Place the mixture in a pan and start with the heat turned up high. Slowly reduce the heat to medium and then down to the lowest level, mixing all the while with a wooden spoon so that it thickens smoothly. This mixture is called Tatara.

You will know when the sauce is ready as the smell of the flour will disappear. Try using a nontraditional methods – don't be afraid to mix using an electric mixer.

Separately, the Tatara, also called Phelamushi, coating can be used by itself to make a perfect dessert – just let it cool and set.

Now, on a thick piece of string, assemble a line of dried apples or nuts. Take the strings and start dipping them slowly into the hot Tatara mixture until well covered. Repeat several times with each one, till you get the desired texture and appearance. The strings of apples or nuts should look like a candle. I prefer making them short for easy consumption and storage. Hang up to dry. When dry they are ready to be stored – but be careful not to wrap them in plastic or they will go mouldy, use a soft cloth.

→ Here in this picture we used several walnut kernels on the string to make it look more authentic and appealing.

BAKED APPLES WITH DRY FRUITS

ვაშლი ღუმელში

This is a true all-season delight. The trick here is that we will add a Georgian touch by stuffing the apples with dry fruits, honey, walnuts and a touch of red wine. For the winter, you can use quinces, which are popular in Georgia.

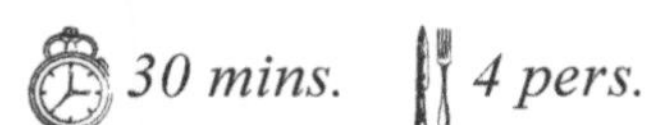 *30 mins.* 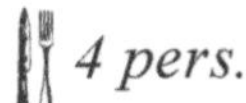 *4 pers.*

Ingredients:
4 green apples;
2 tbsps. of honey;
Vegetable oil or butter
Some dry fruits.

How to prepare:
Preheat the oven to 350 degrees F (175 degrees C) before starting to prepare the apples.
Now take out the cores of the apples or cut out the top half and create a lid, which you can put back on it. Take out the inner core from the top of the apple, leaving a well. Do not cut all the way through. Put in the honey, vegan butter, finely chopped dry fruits of your choice, and a drizzle of wine. Close the lids of the apples, or if you are doing it with the cores taken out, wrap them in foil.
Bake them in the preheated oven for 15 minutes, until the sugar begins to caramelize and the apples are tender.

ACKNOWLEDGEMENTS

For many years I have been entertaining friends from around the globe in my house or at my cooking classes and giving them the chance to try the cuisine of my homeland. It uplifts me to see their happy faces as they try something new, whether it is an evening meal, lunch or just a snack. I love small and cosy dinners, where people talk, discuss global issues, ideas, and why being vegan is good for this planet and what should be done to avoid animal suffering and over-farming.

Not only do I love to cook a wonderful meal for my guests and friends, but I also love to decorate the table with quirky Georgian designs and tricks, with hints of Asian and Oriental ideas. Food and decoration have always struck a chord for me. That beautiful Georgian figurine looks great next to the walnut vegetables, and that tablecloth looks even better alongside a selection of Murabas.

And one of the best things about Georgia and Georgian food is that the cuisine is economical to create. Any big or small supermarket or corner shop can supply everything you need for your recipes to enable you to prepare something simple and yet memorable. Just get some Georgian ingredients and improvise!

The past decade has seen Georgia come into the tourism mainstream and fashion: everywhere you look, tourists are enjoying its nature.
Georgia is also recognised as the historic 'Cradle of Wine' and offers its culinary adventures. So, what will be the future place of Georgia and its ancient capital Tbilisi in international culinary tourism? I truly believe that the prominent place that vegan and vegetarian dishes occupy in its cuisine will win it more international recognition as our world moves towards eating less meat.

My Georgian culinary colleagues - chefs, restaurateurs, managers and brand creators - are with me on this. More and more places are offering strict vegetarian menus and even cakes that are vegan.

My friend and colleague of many years Manana Manjgaladze is something I am not – a person with green fingers. She has an amazing garden, so thanks to her I was intro-

duced and recommended to Zurab Shevardnadze, a genius gardener who revolutionised how Georgians tend their gardens. The cover picture and food pictures were taken in a paradise that I never saw anywhere else before. Thank you Zura!

All the products used in my books, such as fruits, vegetables, honey, cornflour, flour and dry fruits and dishes cooked are made strictly from natural, boutique-style farming, such as Barbale, located in Atskuri, founded by Keti Didmanidze.

Special thanks to the company ''Guruna'' for providing some dry fruits.

I want to thank Betsy, my lifelong - it seems - American friend who loves Georgia as we all should. Betsy and I thoroughly discussed every single dish in her beautiful home-grown garden before writing it down, as we believe that if we can create it, so can you. We want you to feel at ease when cooking Georgian food.

While working on my book, I did quite a lot of driving, travelling and meeting people all over Georgia. Thank you to the company GULF and especially Nino Jibladze for helping by providing eco fuel for my small, environmentally-friendly car. We were a great match.

Once again, the best Georgian brand of tea: Gurieli - Born in Georgia, and its chief Mikheil Chkuaseli. Many thanks to Gurieli for continuing Georgia's tea history and featuring in the book.

Massive thanks to Guram Kiknadze, a young and well-travelled restaurateur, descendant of Abkhazia and expert in its cuisine, wonderful began family member Temur Nikoleishvili and Koka Nikoleishvili, my two naughty brothers who love this planet, wonderful writer Salome Asatiani, who loves Lobio and shares a passion for food and David Lynch with me, Ana Tikaradze, a powerful vegan ideologist in Georgia, considering how unusual it is here, to Meriko Gubeladze for successfully running a vegetarian eatery in the capital, Tbilisi, where tourists find what they are looking for, Teona Bagdavadze, a wonderful PR girl on heels who gave up the glitz and glamour of fur and steak and started eating vegan especially for me, and my family which tolerates my non-meat dinners.The company Guruna for providing some sweet ingredients. I want to thank all my colleagues - journalists, reporters and TV personalities in Georgia and abroad who helped me to promote my previous book, Nino Baratashvili, Tea Agladze, Giorgi Lapherashvili, Nino Darso, George Sharashidze, Maiko Tsereteli, Cate Popkhadze, Misha Robaqidze, Goderdzi Sharashia, the entire TV Pirveli team, Tako Gvazava, Sopho Megrelidze, CNN's remarkable Jill Doherty, Ellen Barry, Svenja O'Donnel, Wendell

Steavenson, Rayhan and Robin, Lawrence Sheets, Matthew Collin for hanging around with me at the Frankfurt Book Fair, Sara Marcus, Nunu Japaridze, Molly Corso, my giant Bloomberg family, all loving my book, the International Women's Association of Georgia with powerful ladies sharing my passion, Roy Southworth, who is no longer with me but forever in our hearts and his wife Cathy Mclain, an unforgettable couple I had a privileged to spend time with in Georgia, Sandra Roelofs, the former First Lady of Georgia, the large Sulakauri Publishing House team, especially Tina and Anna, Eka Sharashidze Voskamp and Gijs Voskamp, Tako Akhaladze, Lali Valois, Daro Sulakauri, Jana Sommerulnd, Marika Eliashvili, Masha Levitov, Valeria Korchagina, Berdia Qamarauli, Agnes Lovasz, Peter Chilvers, Daniel Hamilton and the unknown American tourist lady at the Georgian State Museum who purchased my book and gave me a hug. The idea of simplifying life, for those who want a quick and easy recipe, really works!

Once again, my project was made possible together with the Gastronaut Company, led by Lali Papashvili and Levan Qoqiashvili and their handpicked team. Gastronaut's photographer Emma Matevosyan shares the same passion for food like me while being a mother of three children and a true master of photography in the kitchen. The Gastronauts team, Emma and Helena, will surprise you again and again in the future.

Thank you again to my former Bloomberg colleague Mark Beech who copy-edited the text and made many valuable suggestions.

Helpful Conversions

Both my grandparents, aunt, mother and many Georgians all use approximate ways to measure. Just a pinch, just a small dash, a little bit of, half a glass!
So, this table will help you measure.

1 pinch = (dry) 0.5 gr
1 dash = 1.25 gr
1 teaspoon = (liquid) 5.0 gr
3 teaspoons = 1 tablespoon or 14.3 grams or ½ ounce
65 tablespoons = 1 pound or 453 gr
1 bunch of herbs = 45 -55 grams
1 litre is 1.1 quarts

Notes